MYSTERIES OF SCIENCE

UFOs
THE UNSOLVED MYSTERY

BY CONNIE COLWELL MILLER

Reading Consultant:
Barbara J. Fox
Reading Specialist
North Carolina State University

Content Consultant:
Jerome Clark, Editor
International UFO Reporter
J. Allen Hynek Center for UFO Studies
Chicago, Illinois

Capstone
press
Mankato, Minnesota

Blazers is published by Capstone Press,
151 Good Counsel Drive, P.O. Box 669, Mankato, Minnesota 56002.
www.capstonepress.com

Library of Congress Cataloging-in-Publication Data
Miller, Connie Colwell, 1976–
    UFOs : the unsolved mystery/by Connie Colwell Miller.
    p. cm. — (Blazers. Mysteries of science.)
    Includes bibliographical references and index.
    Summary: "Presents the mystery of UFOs, including current theories and famous
sightings" — Provided by publisher.
    ISBN-13: 978-1-4296-2331-5 (hardcover)
    ISBN-10: 1-4296-2331-4 (hardcover)
    [1. Unidentified flying objects.] I. Title. II. Series.
TL789.M52 2009
001.942 — dc22   2008028697

Editorial Credits
Lori Shores, editor; Alison Thiele, designer; Marcie Spence, photo researcher

Photo Credits
Alamy/Clare Charleson, 28–29; ImageState, cover; Mark Wagner Aviation-Images, 4–5; Mary
    Evans Picture Library, 8–9, 18–19, 24; Stock Connection Blue, 6–7
Corbis/Bettmann, 12–13, 25
Fortean Picture Library, 10–11
Getty Images Inc./Popperfoto, 22–23; STR/AFP, 26–27
Newscom, 14; Solent News/Splash News and Pictures, 15
Shutterstock/Marilyn Volan, grunge background (throughout); Maugli, 16–17 (background);
    Michael Ledray, 20–21; rgbspace, (paper art element) 3, 17; Shmeliova Natalia, 16 (paper art
    element)

TABLE OF CONTENTS

FLYING
OBJECT

In May 1995, John Waller
saw a long row of white lights.
They blinked in the sky ahead
of his airplane.

Waller called air traffic controllers in Albuquerque, New Mexico. The controllers didn't see anything unusual on the **radar**.

radar — equipment that uses radio waves to track the location of objects

UFO FACT

UFO stands for Unidentified Flying Object.

Lightning suddenly lit up the sky. Waller saw a long **aircraft**. Waller had seen a UFO.

aircraft — a vehicle that can fly

Many UFO researchers think this 1951 photo is a fake.

WHAT ARE UFOs?

A UFO is an object in the sky that can't be explained. Some UFOs look like aircraft. Others are only flashing lights.

UFO FACT

According to a 2002 study, one in seven Americans say they or someone they know has seen a UFO.

UFO FACT

About 70,000 UFOs are reported each year. There are about 192 sightings each day.

People all over the world report UFO **sightings**. Many people have seen strange discs or triangles. Round and cigar-shaped UFOs are also common.

sighting — an experience of seeing something

Alien spaceships attack Earth in the movie *Independence Day*.

Some people think that UFOs are spaceships from other planets. These people believe that **aliens** are visiting Earth.

alien — a creature from another planet

Filmmakers have created some scary
aliens, like this one from the movie *Alien 3*.

FAMOUS SIGHTINGS

- In January 2008, people in Stephenville, Texas, saw many large aircraft with flashing lights. The objects flew lower than airplanes. Many people think they were from another planet.

- Something crashed near Roswell, New Mexico, in July 1947. People reported seeing a disc-shaped UFO before the crash. The U.S. government says the UFO was just a weather balloon.

In July 2007, people in the United Kingdom looked up in shock. Four lights glowed in the sky. Three of the lights flew together to form a triangle. No one knows what the lights were.

Hundreds of people saw something strange in Phoenix, Arizona, in March 1997. Bright lights formed a triangle in the sky. The military said they were flares. But no one knows for sure.

Fred and Phyll Dickeson took this picture of a UFO in New Zealand.

EXPLAINING UFOs

Many scientists find ways to explain UFOs. These scientists think people mistake bright stars or planets for aircraft.

Many UFOs turn out to be airplanes, birds, or even large groups of insects. Unusual weather conditions also explain some UFO sightings.

UFO FACT

Some UFOs are fakes. People have used balloons with lights in them to fool others.

Some UFO sightings have never been explained. These **mysterious** events make people wonder if UFOs could be alien spaceships.

mysterious — very hard to explain or understand

This picture was taken in Salem, Massachusetts, in 1952.

FLYING SAUCERS:

AN ANALYSIS OF THE
AIR FORCE
PROJECT BLUE BOOK
SPECIAL REPORT No. 14

INCLUDING
THE C.I.A. AND THE SAUCERS

PREPARED BY
DR. LEON DAVIDSON

FIFTH EDITION
DECEMBER, 1976

UFO FACT

Many people think world leaders
know more about UFOs than
they are telling us.

In 1947, members of the U.S. Air Force began looking for answers to UFOs. They interviewed many people and looked at UFO pictures. But they did not solve the mystery.

THE FUTURE OF UFOs

Researchers have gathered thousands of UFO pictures and drawings. But no one has proven that UFOs are from another planet.

Maybe one day we will know the truth about UFOs. Until then, people will wonder about these strange objects in the sky.

UFO FACT

Every year, about 200,000 people visit the International UFO Museum and Research Center in Roswell, New Mexico.

GLOSSARY

aircraft (AIR-kraft) — a vehicle that can fly

alien (AY-lee-uhn) — a creature from another planet

flare (FLAYR) — a burst of light shot from a gun

interview (IN-tur-vyoo) — to ask someone questions to find out more about something

mysterious (miss-TIHR-ee-uhss) — very hard to explain or understand

planet (PLAN-it) — a large object that moves around a star; the Earth is a planet.

radar (RAY-dar) — equipment that uses radio waves to track the location of objects

scientist (SYE-un-tist) — a person who studies science

sighting (SITE-ing) — an experience of seeing something

READ MORE

Grace, N. B. *UFO Mysteries.* Boys Rock! Chanhassen, Minn.: Child's World, 2007.

Grace, N. B. *UFOs: What Scientists Say May Shock You!* 24/7: Behind the Scenes. New York: Franklin Watts, 2008.

Oxlade, Chris. *The Mystery of UFOs.* Can Science Solve? Chicago: Heinemann, 2006.

INTERNET SITES

FactHound offers a safe, fun way to find educator-approved Internet sites related to this book.

Here's what you do:

1. Visit *www.facthound.com*
2. Choose your grade level.
3. Begin your search.

This book's ID number is 9781429623315.

FactHound will fetch the best sites for you!

INDEX